365 Powerful Positive Affirmations for Black Women

Reprogram Your Mind to Boost Confidence,
Self-Esteem, Attract Success, Make Money,
Health, and Love

Layla Moon

i

Table of Contents

4 FREE Gifts

To help you along your spiritual journey, I've created 4 FREE bonus eBooks.

You can get instant access by signing up to my email newsletter below.

On top of the 4 free books, you will also receive weekly tips along with free book giveaways, discounts, and so much more.

All of these bonuses are 100% free with no strings attached. You don't need to provide any personal information except your email address.

To get your bonus, go to:

https://dreamlifepress.com/four-free-gifts

Or scan the QR code below

Spirit Guides for Beginners: How to Hear the Universe's Call and Communicate with Your Spirit Guide and Guardian Angels

Guided by Moon herself, inspired by her own experiences and knowledge that has been passed down by hundreds of generations for thousands of years, you'll discover everything you need to know to;

- Understanding what the call of the universe is
- How to hear and comprehend it
- Knowing who and what your spirit guides and guardian angels are
- Learning how to connect, start a conversation, and listen to your guides
- How to manifest your dreams with the help of the cosmic source
- Learning how to start living the life you want to live
- And so much more…

Law of Attraction: Manifest Your Desire

Learn how to tap into the infinite power of the universe and manifest everything you want in life.

Includes:

- Law of Attraction: Manifest Your Desire ebook
- Law of Attraction Workbook
- Cheat sheets and checklists so make sure you're on the right path

Hoodoo Book of Spells for Beginners: Easy and effective Rootwork, Conjuring, and Protection Spells for Healing and Prosperity

Harness the power of one of the greatest magics. Hoodoo is a powerful force ideal for holding negativity at bay, promoting positivity in all areas in your life, offering protection to the things you love, and ultimately taking control of your destiny.

Inside, you will discover:
- How to get started with Hoodoo in your day-to-day life
- How to use conjuration spells to manifest the life you want to live
- How casting protection spells can help you withstand the toughest of times
- Break cycles of bad luck and promote good fortune throughout your life
- Hoodoo to encourage prosperity and financial stability
- How to heal using Hoodoo magic, both short-term and long-term traumas and troubles
- Remove curses and banish pain, suffering, and negativity from your life
- And so much more…

Book of Shadows

A printable PDF to support you in your spiritual transformation.

Within the pages, you will find:

- Potion and tinctures tracking sheet
- Essential oils log pages
- Herbs log pages
- Magical rituals and spiritual body goals checklist
- Tarot reading spread sheets
- Weekly moon and planetary cycle tracker
- And so much more

Get all the resources for FREE by visiting the link below

https://dreamlifepress.com/four-free-gifts

Introduction

Nobody starts out hating who they are. This is something that you are socially programmed to do. We enter this world innocent and pure. The concept of race, gender, and social norms are taught to us. In a perfect world, your beautiful inner self is acknowledged from the second you enter this world. But since we live in a cruel place that teaches love is pain and that beauty is painted, we tend to see ourselves through other people's eyes. Sadly, what is reflected is an image that is far from who we are.

In my early teens and well into my late 20s, I looked for myself in the media. It was rare to find a woman who looked like me. The aesthetic for the ideal black women included features I didn't naturally possess and because of this, I never felt beautiful enough. People in my family called me beautiful but I always thought that they were obligated to say that because they were family. I never felt genuinely pretty. At least not until I was able to afford the surgical enhancements that would transform me into the "beautiful" black women I saw on screen and in my favorite magazines.

My inability to accept myself was not limited to looks. In relationships, I felt the need to talk and behave in a certain way so that my "blackness" didn't jump out at peopleI won't even touch the racial biases at work.

I grew up thinking that I could only be the best version of myself if I was anyone but me. Does this sound familiar? It is heartbreaking, but a lot of women of color identify with the picture I just painted. We push ourselves to fit the "acceptable" narrative at a price that is too steep - our identity.

It was somewhere on this journey that I found the courage to silence the voices around me and look inward. What I found there was pretty amazing. I discovered that I actually liked myself! This was a shocking revelation for me and the deeper I delved in, the harder I fell for my quirky sense of humor, my kinky black hair, and my not so curvy body. I wish I could say that this self-love happened overnight. It was a long drawn-out process with occasional setbacks (what superhero movie doesn't have that epic setback?). The result is this powerfully confident black woman (aka Moi) blazing trails in her workplace, successfully breaking through corporate ceilings, and currently typing furiously at her computer to ensure that other black women get to live up to their true and full potential.

Affirmations played a huge role in my transformation journey. I used my words to echo the beauty I found inside and this helped me gain confidence. The more confident I was, the farther away I drifted from my comfort zone. And as you probably know, growth happens outside the comfort zone; and with growth comes success in life.

I started with one phrase at a time. Telling myself things like, "I can do this," "I am capable," and so on were helpful but very generic at the time. So, I stepped things up by personalizing those phrases and that was when the magic began.

My tough to maintain hair became my crown. My body became more than just lines and curves but a vessel to carry divinity. With this change in perception came a change in behavior and thinking. It felt sacrilegious to think, say, or do anything about or to myself that was remotely negative. It is shocking to think that a few months prior, I was ready to go under the knife. Whatever your role is in life or wherever your journey has taken you, it is never too late or too early to start disconnecting yourself from the negative social conditioning that characterized your experiences. You don't have to be who they say you are. The only person you should be is yourself.

Becoming yourself is simply that; be who you are. We don't have a template or manual to refer to, so we get the added bonus of creating the person we want to be and speaking those words to ourselves until we embody this new truth. That is exactly what we are going to do in this book. The affirmations I share here are the ones that resonated with, and worked for, me. You can use this as a starting point and then as you grow, personalize it until you have created the life you want.

You just need to make sure that:

1. You are consistent with your affirmations.

This applies to the frequency of your affirmations and your ability to stay true to the words you speak. Here is an example of what I mean; you may tell yourself that you are beautiful and a few moments later, some random dude calls you, "an ugly fat bitch." This hurts especially if you have struggled with accepting yourself. However, your job is to ensure that you counteract this by remaining consistent in affirming your beauty.

Never hold onto the lies that other people tell you. Often, it is not about you. They are most likely projecting their self-loathing and insecurities onto you. The only words that matter are the ones you tell yourself. Be consistent in speaking the right words. In the face of that "ugly fat bitch" comment, tell the world that you are a confident badass bitch with the heart, soul, and body of a goddess.

2. You believe in what you say

For the longest time, I found it difficult to accept the phrase, 'I am amazing.' It felt like I was bragging.

Sometimes, I felt like I was talking about someone else... someone who looked like me. It wasn't until I internalized this message that I started experiencing its impact. Even when I was thrust into situations that made me doubt my efficiency, it was easy for me to remind myself of the fact that I am truly amazing.

When you start your affirmations, you are going to struggle with accepting what you are saying because of years of negative programming. But when you hold fast, it becomes a fact, and the moment you believe in the words you speak, your affirmations become manifestations.

3. You are positive

To create a positive environment within, you must cultivate a positive attitude especially towards your affirmations. This doesn't mean that won't have negative feelings. Those emotions come naturally to us. However, you cannot act or speak based on those emotions. When you recite your affirmations, do it from a place of positivity. Truly believe in the words you are saying and see yourself becoming that person.

One of the easiest ways I learned to do that was by

picturing myself a few years from where the moment I am in. In this vision, I remove limitations and negative experiences and just focus on what it would be like to be the person I want to be. This creates a feeling that activates the positive energy you need for your affirmations.

Now that we have gotten this out of the way, let us get into the affirmations. You are free to use them however you wish. The key is to remain consistent, committed, and to stand in your conviction. Remember, the transformation is not going to happen overnight and just because you aren't seeing physical evidence of your affirmations doesn't mean that they are not working. You need to keep saying them regardless of what is going on in your life.

Having said that, let me give you a quick breakdown of the structure of the book. There are five chapters with at least 70 affirmations per chapter. Each affirmation is meant to be spoken each day. But there is no harm in repeating affirmations multiple times a day or reciting more than one affirmation a day. If it resonates with you and aligns with your vision, tap into its power. Speak them boldly. Speak them out loud. Speak them with absolute confidence.

CHAPTER ONE

Unlearn the Past

The past, they say, shapes our future. Many of us come from troubled pasts, and to move into a desired future, we need to break the chains that hold us back. One of the strongest links in the chains is the horrible lies we have been fed about ourselves. Break that link and the whole house of cards comes crumbling down.

In this chapter, you are going to unlearn every lie you have been told.

1. I am my own person. I am not the mistake of the

people who came before me.

2. I live for myself. My purpose is not to meet the expectations or ideals of others.

3. I am going to be me. I don't need to be anybody else to make it in this life.

4. My dark skin and kinky hair are hallmarks of my beauty.

5. The lines and curves of my body are like sirens. They announce my presence to the world.

6. My attitude is my beauty sauce. I don't need to "act right" to be considered beautiful.

7. I decide the blueprint for who I want to be. I refuse to be defined by what society thinks I should be.

8. I am making my own path in life. I am not bound to repeat the sins of my parents.

9. I am expressing my freedom in my words, thoughts, and actions. I am not a slave to my history.

10. I am a queen. Period. No negative label defines me and the way I live my life.

11. I belong to me. I own my body. I decide what is best for me.

12. I am a winner in everything I do. I am not a victim.

13. My opinions, thoughts, and feelings matter. I deserve to be heard.

14. I am a valuable member of society. I am precious and a treasure.

15. My contribution to society goes beyond social constructs about my worth.

16. I am powerful. My gender does not put a limit on my potential.

17. Being black is not a flaw. It is a fraction of my identity that I am super proud of.

18. I am made for greatness. My current environment or circumstance does not define my future.

19. Where I come from does not dictate where I am going.

20. I will always win. I will not be defeated by the challenges stacked up against me.

21. I have absolute confidence in myself. Other people's doubts cannot bring me down.

22. I am an exceptional woman. I am not defined by the racial stereotypes imposed on me.

23. Being a black woman doesn't make me less. It gives me the edge I need to thrive.

24. I know who I am. I don't need to prove myself to anyone.

25. My actions, words, and opinions do not define the degree of my blackness.

26. I am a strong woman. I am not prey or victim for people to take advantage of.

27. I am precious. I deserve to be loved and protected by the people in my world.

28. I am wise. I make decisions that have a positive impact on me and my community.

29. I work hard. I am neither lazy nor complacent.

30. I am a heroine in my life. I am not waiting to be rescued.

31. I take responsibility for my actions. I am not a product or victim of society.

32. I am a wealth creator. I break any cycle of poverty in my family.

33. I am a wealth manager. I convert my resources into generational wealth.

34. I am a woman of principle. This does not make me difficult to work with.

35. I am passionate and vocal. I am not angry or bitter.

36. I always stand up for what is right. My gender or race will not be used to silence me.

37. I am rewriting my past, not repeating my mistakes.

38. I am bold. I refuse to live in the shadow of fear caused by society's misconceptions about me based on the color of my skin.

39. I am breaking through every glass ceiling in my work, love, and social life.

40. I am a deliberate success. I didn't stumble into my wealth. I created it.

41. I am confident in my sexuality. This does not make me promiscuous or loose.

42. I have strong family values. I am positively building my home.

43. I am actively prioritizing my mental health. I do what is right for me.

44. I am giving myself a chance to heal from past trauma. I am done lugging my pain around.

45. I choose the right relationships for me. The cycle of pain, abuse, and betrayal is over.

46. I know and recognize true love. I know that pain does not mean love.

47. I am loved. I naturally gravitate towards people who genuinely love and mean me well.

48. I am not ashamed of who I was and where I come from.

49. I am protected. I am sheltered. I am not prey to anyone who wants to harm me.

50. In the face of challenges, I am defiant.

51. I am a woman of distinct pedigree and grace. Neither my past nor my present reality can change this.

52. Life is working out in my favor.

53. I have strong willpower. I will not be manipulated into making bad decisions.

54. I am everything I said I would be, and I have exceeded every limitation placed on me by society.

55. I bear the marks and scars on my body with pride. They tell the story of my origin and how far I have come.

56. I am normalizing healthy family relationships that promote positivity and mental well-being.

57. I am breaking the silent covenant that allows abuse and pain to be the norm.

58. I am focused on healing. I refuse to bleed on people who did not hurt me.

59. I am acting from a place of love and compassion.

60. I am letting go of guilt and shame. I forgive myself for my past mistakes.

61. I am walking with my head held high. My past has lost its hold on me.

62. I am cutting ties with my abusers.

63. I live by my own code. Not some misguided sense of duty or loyalty.

64. I am choosing the people who choose me and not people who feel entitled to my time.

65. I am not governed by the pain inflicted on me.

66. I am made for love and not just someone else's pleasure.

67. I am surrounded by abundant opportunities.

68. I am proud of the woman I am and the woman I am becoming.

69. I love my features. I don't need to change them to "fit in."

70. I am choosing my happiness from this day forward.

71. I am life.

72. I am divine.

73. I am light.

CHAPTER TWO

Affirm Your Truth

The world may say terrible things about you. The people you love may say hurtful things to you about yourself - sometimes not deliberately. Even your actions may betray your true intentions, leading you to question or doubt yourself. But none of these matter as much as the words you speak to yourself.

The truth is a strong powerful force capable of breaking through walls of lies. The more you live in the light of the truth, the harder it is for darkness to dim this light. Affirm your truth and manifest your potential and desires.

1. I am powerful. I can handle the storm that rages in life.

2. I am beautiful inside and out. My beauty transcends the physical form.

3. I am courageous. I am not afraid to stand by what I believe.

4. I am a woman of integrity. I live by values that cannot be compromised.

5. I am intelligent. I make very smart decisions in life.

6. I am kind. I extend mercy and compassion to those who need it.

7. I am my sister's keeper. I love seeing the women around me succeed.

8. I am a woman of my word. I keep every promise and respect my vows.

9. I am important. I matter to a lot of people in this world.

10. I am worthy. I deserve all the love, peace, and happiness.

11. I am capable. I set out to accomplish every task I assign to myself.

12. I am dependable. I can be counted on to do my part in any situation.

13. I am forgiving. I don't hold grudges or harbor hatred for anyone.

14. I am patient. I think strategically before taking action.

15. I am loyal. I pitch my tent with those deserving of my loyalty.

16. I am royalty. I wear my crown with grace and wisdom.

17. I am talented. My creativity and resourcefulness know no boundaries.

18. I am safe. I am constantly surrounded by people who support and protect me.

19. I am present. I am not lost in past glories or chasing futile dreams.

20. I am free. My skin color, tax bracket, or past sins

cannot slow me down.

21. I am assertive. I am no pushover or anyone's plaything.

22. I am in love. I love my life and the people I allow into my space.

23. I own myself. I am not controlled or manipulated by anyone.

24. I am successful. I am rich in resources and in my finances.

25. I am healthy. I experience renewed vitality in my body every day.

26. I am connected. I know my history and I am not ashamed of my roots.

27. I am magical. My skin color adds an extra layer of beauty that makes me amazing.

28. I am strong. I am built to outlast tough times.

29. I am sexy. I embrace my sexuality and acknowledge the power of my sensuality.

30. I am amazing. Every day, I conquer my fears and make great things happen.

31. I am unbreakable. I may stumble. I may fall. But I always rise back up.

32. I am irresistible. The right people are attracted to my many amazing qualities.

33. I am unique. There is only one me in the entire universe and I am proud of her.

34. I am clean. I engage in practices that honor my body physically, mentally, and spiritually.

35. I regret nothing. I learn from my mistakes, pick myself up, and move forward.

36. I am the best version of myself and the only one better than me is the woman I am becoming.

37. I am extra; extraordinary, extroverted, and extralogical.

38. I am peaceful. My words and actions are reflections of my peaceful nature.

39. I am passionate. I am very excited about my work,

my life, and my love.

40. I am hopeful. I know that the future I want will become my reality.

41. I am devout. I stand for what I believe with honesty and courage.

42. I am divine. I pay homage to the goddess within by loving and respecting myself.

43. I am a nurturer. People feel loved and at peace whenever they come into contact with me.

44. I am genuine. I live a life that is true to my core values.

45. I am perceptive. I have a well-developed sixth sense and I intuitively know what is right for me.

46. I am disciplined. I am guided by principles that allow me to stay on the path leading to my goals.

47. I am in control. I have absolute power over my emotions and my tongue.

48. I am proactive. I am not reactive. I anticipate correctly and take the appropriate action.

49. I am a doer. I don't build castles in the air. I support my words with action.

50. I am a giver. I am generous with my time, my love, and my wealth.

51. I am driven. I am strongly self-motivated and strive to reach my goals every day.

52. I am ambitious. My desire to succeed takes me out of my comfort and into my area of growth.

53. I am happy. I chase my dreams, but I appreciate the joys of the present.

54. I am affectionate. I am not afraid to speak of or show my love to the people I care about.

55. I am persistent. When I set my mind on something, I go after it until it is done.

56. I am resilient. I can persevere through challenges with fierce determination.

57. I am black. For me, that means more melanin, more magic, and more magnificence.

58. I am majestic. I walk with pride, stand with

confidence, and talk with grace.

59. I am positively glowing. My skin, my hair, and my body reflect my inner joy.

60. I am independent. I don't need anyone's permission to live my life.

61. I am captivating. I am not the kind of woman people meet and forget.

62. I am a rebel. I have no problem following the rules. I just appreciate my life better on my terms.

63. I am good. And I get better every day.

64. I am bold. I don't bow to my fears or give up on myself.

65. I am gold. I am valuable and I know my worth.

66. I am peculiar. I embrace and celebrate my distinction.

67. I am me. And I will never change that for anybody.

68. I am a hero. I get up every day and show up for myself regardless of the challenges.

69. I am favored. I am given preferential treatment wherever I go.

70. I am loved. The people in my inner circle have genuine appreciation and love for me.

71. I am blessed. I have everything I need to succeed in this life.

72. I am respected. My opinions and contributions at home and work are valued.

73. I am productive. I make the most of my time and my resources.

CHAPTER THREE

Embrace Your Power

Every woman is born with an innate power that makes her seem extraordinary. If you have ever seen a bear or lioness defend their cub, you know the power I am talking about. It is the kind of power that makes you look at the source of your fear in the eye and still take that bold step anyway. It changes the course of history and creates a ripple effect that lasts generations into the future.

Some of us have been raised to believe that the only power we have as black women is between our legs. Honey, that is just one aspect of our power. Over the next 73 days, you are going to acknowledge that power, channel it, and use it to manifest the life you want.

1. I have the seeds of nations within me. I birth empires and dynasties.

2. I am a kingmaker. I choose my life partner diligently.

3. I am a world-class leader. I serve with purpose and lead with confidence.

4. I am a multi-millionaire. I turn my ideas into successful brands.

5. I am the complete package. I bring abundance to the table.

6. I am exceptional. Mediocrity is not a word in my book.

7. I am a businesswoman. I recognize opportunities and successfully monetize them.

8. I am a team player. I play a crucial role in any team I am a part of.

9. I am a goal-getter. I am the one people call on when they want to get the job done.

10. I am evolving. I grow in every aspect of my life.

11. I am charismatic. I can charm and talk my way out of anything.

12. I am gifted. My skills and talents are sought after by top-rated companies.

13. I am focused. I keep my eye on the prize and my feet on the path to my dreams.

14. I am a chart breaker. I am pushing past limitations and braving new frontiers.

15. I am a woman with power. I make the decisions that matter the most in my life.

16. I am a positive influencer. I raise the stock of anything or anyone I associate with.

17. I am socially strategic. I build alliances and partnerships with the right kind of people.

18. I am spiritually sound. My faith and beliefs are firmly rooted in my convictions.

19. I am vocal. I eloquently communicate my thoughts and feelings.

20. I am enough. I do not need outside validation to build my self-esteem.

21. I am the prize. Anyone I consider good enough to date or marry is lucky.

22. I am solution oriented. I am turning every stumbling block in my way into steppingstones.

23. I am a survivor. I am thriving and rising above every attempt to ruin my life.

24. I am physically fit. I am of sound mind and body and I maintain a healthy routine that keeps them that way.

25. I am a visioner. I dream powerful dreams and put in the work to make them a reality.

26. I am a cheerleader. I love to see the people in my circle succeed and I do my part to cheer them on.

27. I am a peacemaker. I have found a way to get along with everyone, including those with biases against me.

28. I am my biggest competition. Every day presents an

opportunity for me to be better than my previous self.

29. I am a changemaker. I lend my voice to the millions of voices seeking to make this world a better place.

30. I am a radical thinker. I think outside the proverbial box.

31. I am a pacesetter. I am actively paving a way for the women who come after me in this generation and the next.

32. I am a provider. I have no problems ensuring that the people I love are taken care of.

33. I am a protector. I create an atmosphere that makes people around me feel protected and safe.

34. I am a builder. I turn every resource at my disposal into desirable assets.

35. I am a global brand. I build locally but I am thriving globally.

36. I am an innovator. I am developing ideas that serve the community around me.

37. I am daring. I don't allow circumstances, past experiences, and outside opinions to shape my dreams.

38. I am a hustler. I work hard, I work smart, and I am always in the winner's lane.

39. I am an intellectual. I look for knowledge and constantly seek out ways to improve myself.

40. I am entrepreneurial. I consider the business opportunities in my environment and seize them.

41. I am virtuous. I know my values and I have no problems upholding them.

42. I am a generous giver. I never abandon anyone who needs my help.

43. I am perceptive. I have the power to accurately sense the right course of action.

44. I am a warrior. I fight for what is right to protect myself and the ones I care for.

45. I am a manager. I manage resources and

relationships to maximize potential.

46. I am a winner. I am a thriving, flourishing woman of substance.

47. I am self-aware. I know who I am, and I am deliberately working on who I become.

48. I am a woman of purpose. I know why I am here, and I live for that purpose.

49. I am a listener. I pay attention to the needs and counsel of the people around me.

50. I am self-reliant. I cannot be bribed or manipulated into doing what I don't want.

51. I am a boss. I create employment opportunities and turn ideas into profitable ventures.

52. I am righteous. I have sound morals and an active conscience that keeps me in check.

53. I am a fighter. I push past my challenges to reach my goal.

54. I am a healer. I strive to maintain peak physical and mental health.

55. I love freely. The scope of my love is not limited by fear or other negative emotions.

56. I am phenomenal. My life is exceptionally amazing in every way.

57. I am sexy. I pleasure myself and my partner in any consensual arrangement.

58. I am a mentor. I have created a success template that others can replicate.

59. I am honorable. Guilt, shame, and past failures cannot stop me from living right.

60. I am dangerous. To anyone who seeks my downfall, I am a thorn in their side.

61. I am strong-willed. I have a stubborn focus that makes me formidable in any arena.

62. I am fearless. I boldly go after what I want every single day.

63. I am fierce. I love and give myself to deserving people passionately.

64. I am a multitasker. I can efficiently handle multiple

projects at once.

65. I am a homemaker. I can turn any living space into a warm haven.

66. I am connected. I have a network of friends and associates who are critical to my business and career growth.

67. I am a temple. I experience divinity through my body.

68. I am a first-class citizen. I am treated well and respected in any environment I find myself in.

69. I am baggage-free. I am over any emotional heartbreak and ready to welcome love.

70. I am whole. I have everything I need to enjoy life to the fullest.

71. I am independent. I don't need anyone's permission to live life on my terms.

72. I am prosperous. I can rely on my net worth to fund my lifestyle.

73. I am perfect. I am everything I need to be to win in this life.

CHAPTER FOUR

Affirmations of Self-Love

It is almost impossible to receive and appreciate genuine love unless you find it within yourself first. In this chapter, these affirmations will take you on a journey that starts with removing the blindfolds brought on by poor self-perception so that the inner vision is activated. This will help you to see yourself in the true light and fall in love with the person revealed.

1. Life has given me a clean slate to start over. I embrace it.

2. I am not the mistakes I have made.

3. I am not the mistakes made by other people.

4. I am a brand-new person; made in my image.

5. I am setting my own standards of beauty.

6. I am done waiting for others to model beauty for me.

7. I embrace everything that makes me a woman.

8. My womanity is my biggest strength.

9. My body is sacred.

10. My heart is a treasure.

11. My pleasure is a priority.

12. Every line, curve, and scar on my body is a tribute to my womanhood.

13. My features are my identity, and I am proud of them.

14. My dark skin is my beauty mark and I treasure it.

15. My hair is my crown and glory. I respect it.

16. My style is my signature. I am bold with it.

17. My smile is captivating. It turns strangers into friends.

18. My accent pays homage to my roots. I am not ashamed of this.

19. My skin color does not determine my trajectory in life.

20. I am comfortable being me.

21. The woman I see in the mirror inspires me every day.

22. I don't aspire to be fixed. My goal is to be better.

23. I prioritize my health because I am worth it.

24. My body houses my mind, my divinity, and my identity. I treasure it.

25. I am both lucky and blessed to have this black woman's body.

26. I celebrate the diversity among my fellow black sisters.

27. My scars, folds, and bumps are not flaws. They are evidence that my body working hard to keep me together.

28. I am flawlessly gorgeous.

29. Today is me-day! I am celebrating my awesomeness.

30. I am deserving of all the good things in life.

31. I am reaching for the stars simply because I can.

32. I cannot get over how beautiful I am.

33. I choose self-expression over public approval. I choose me.

34. I am attracting the right relationships into my life. I deserve it.

35. I love the woman I am today the same way I love the woman I will become tomorrow.

36. I express self-love freely and without hesitation.

37. I am celebrating every milestone and victory; big and small.

38. I am patient with my journey of growth.

39. I am taking more chances on myself today.

40. I am shutting out any negative voice in my life.

41. I am cutting ties with anyone who takes pleasure in my pain. I deserve better.

42. I reject relationships that undermine my worth.

43. I see the best in me every time.

44. I am amazing, and nobody can make me think otherwise.

45. I am surrounding myself with positivity and love.

46. I am done tolerating people who hurt me in the name of love. I deserve wholesome relationships.

47. I am bold enough to walk away from anyone who disrespects me.

48. I embrace every facet of myself, and I find comfort in that.

49. I am working hard at being better and I am enjoying the process.

50. I am committed to this new relationship I have with myself.

51. I will never give up on myself.

52. My humanity and all that it implies does not make me less amazing.

53. I am in pursuit of dreams that help me live my best life.

54. I acknowledge the progress I am making to become better.

55. I will not put myself down to make anyone feel better.

56. I am light. I don't need to dim the light of other people just so I can shine.

57. I embrace my history; my failures, my mistakes, and my regrets. But they can never define my future.

58. I walk in absolute freedom. I am free from the burden of self-hatred.

59. I renounce every form of self-sabotage. I am committed to my success.

60. I am precious, and I show this in the way I treat myself.

61. I am taking away the right for anyone to treat me less than I deserve.

62. I want love, respect, and compassion. I refuse to settle for less.

63. I am in a healthy relationship with myself. I am putting in the work to make this relationship durable.

64. I am partnering with people who are interested in my growth.

65. I am removing every limitation I have placed on myself. I am capable of great things.

66. I am taking advantage of every opportunity that helps me elevate myself.

67. I am done taking actions that procrastinate my happiness. I am going after what I want.

68. My self-worth is not rooted in the approval of outsiders. It is in my self-approval.

69. I know who I am. And that is enough for me.

70. I am satisfied with who I am right now. But I am also invested in the person I want to be tomorrow.

71. I am content with not "fitting in" as long as I am authentic.

72. I am living my life with all my might.

73. I am stepping out of my shell and living as my true self.

CHAPTER FIVE

Affirmations for Confidence

The courage to live your life to its fullest potential requires extraordinary confidence. If you are fortunate enough to have a primary support unit that has fed you with words that affirmed your confidence since your early years, that is fantastic. You are several steps into your journey already. If this is not the case for you, that is okay.

In this chapter, you will unlock your confidence and build yourself to a point where you become immune to the negative messages that make up your programming.

1. I am that badass bitch that everyone wants in their corner.

2. In the arena of public opinion, I choose to focus on myself.

3. I am selfish with my time. I refuse to waste it on things that don't serve me.

4. I am effortlessly achieving my goals today.

5. No number of naysayers can break me down.

6. I am rocking my skin and everything it incorporates with pride.

7. Nothing can stop me from winning today.

8. I am Ms. Capable. I get the job done no matter what.

9. I am ready for today. I was built for it.

10. I can achieve whatever I set my mind to.

11. I am a woman on a mission. I cannot be stopped.

12. I am irreplaceable. My work and results can only be replicated by me.

13. I am the standard. I am not trying to be anyone else.

14. I am made unique and distinct. There is no one else like me.

15. I am an exceptional black woman. I am far from ordinary.

16. I am done putting in the minimum effort. I am all about maximizing.

17. I am confident in who I am, and I am not afraid to stand out as long as I stay true to myself.

18. I refuse to be small. I unleash every potential hidden within me.

19. I am living beyond the boundaries and limitations of societal expectations.

20. My time has come. I am conquering every fear that has held me back and stepping into the light.

21. I dream big dreams and I am daring in my attempts

to make them my reality.

22. I am not afraid to succeed. I am adequately built to handle the life of success.

23. I am not living to survive. I am committed to thriving and flourishing.

24. My existence is essential. I am not an accident or a mistake. I am destined to play a critical role in life.

25. I believe in who I am and in the purpose that backs my existence. I will fulfill my destiny.

26. I accept total responsibility for how I use the resources at my disposal. I am choosing to use them to achieve my dreams.

27. The failures in my past cannot mask or deny the potential I have. I choose to focus on my potential.

28. I am channeling my energy and mental resources into personal development. The more I grow, the more confident I become.

29. I silence any voice that promotes my failures and weaknesses over my triumphs and strengths.

30. I am mentally programmed for success. I am built to live a life characterized by exceptional brilliance.

31. The only person capable of denying my dreams is me

and I am done being my own obstacle. Therefore, nothing stands in my way.

32. Today, I am confidently taking the right steps to achieve my goals. I am checking off my to-do lists effortlessly.

33. I am boldly charging onward and forward. The fear that imprisoned and immobilized me has lost its power.

34. I refuse to settle for mediocrity. My mind and mental prowess are expanding beyond the limits placed on me by fear, negativity, and social expectations.

35. I am not settling for the glories of the past. Every day, I am pushing myself to be better so that I can achieve even greater things.

36. My journey is not about perfection. It is about making progress. Every day, I am getting better.

37. My race, my gender, and my age cannot stop me from maximizing my potential. I am made of more.

38. My propensity for attaining greatness is not locked in my DNA or ancestry. It is a mindset thing and I have the right mindset to achieve the level of greatness I aspire to.

39. I was born for a time like this. I was created for days that demand excellence and maximum effort.

40. I am carrying out my tasks diligently and efficiently. I strike with precision and follow with determination.

41. I refuse to give up my goals because of social or environmental restrictions. I am pushing past any obstacles to claim my prize.

42. Today, I choose to give my all... to express myself fully in terms of my work and to go beyond the expectations of others in my delivery.

43. I embrace my capacity to do and be more than what is expected of me. I refuse to live a life that is influenced, altered, or determined by the opinions of others.

44. I refuse to devalue or demean my worth by comparing myself with anyone else. I am my only competition, and my goal is to be better than the person I was yesterday.

45. I am stepping out of the shadows where social biases based on my gender and race have kept me. I am entering into the light of who I truly am.

46. In my quest to fulfill my potential as a black woman of excellence, I am not leaving any stones unturned.

47. There are not enough "Nos" in the world to knock me off my A-game. I have a titanium-grade confidence that simply brushes it off and keeps moving.

48. I embrace my failures. They highlight the flaws in my methods and unlock the next step I am supposed to take.

49. I know what I want, and I am confident enough to strategically pursue it to its expected conclusion.

50. Today, I am boldly venturing into new territories to explore new possibilities for myself. I am stepping out

of my comfort zone.

51. I embrace the changes that come with each season in life because I know that I am capable of adapting.

52. My outward experiences cannot dictate my internal atmosphere. I find happiness, love, and courage within.

53. My ability to succeed today is not determined by my past experiences. I win because I have decided to.

54. I am casting aside anything and anyone that attempts to diminish my confidence.

55. I am altering my value system, principles, and priorities to reflect my new direction in life.

56. I am attracting and connecting with the kind of people or circumstances that elevate me mentally, physically, and financially.

57. I am letting go of habits, thoughts, practices, and beliefs that poison my ability to believe in myself.

58. I am taking the time to rebuild my confidence and establish my self-worth. No one can ever take this from me.

59. I have absolute faith in myself and what I am capable of. This inspires the confidence I need to succeed.

60. I have a strong network of friends and family who support my growth without feeling threatened by my confidence.

61. I know the resources I have for reaching my goals and I am not hesitant in making the most out of them.

62. I am not a helpless woman waiting to be rescued. I

am a mistress of strategy and master of implementing it to change my fate.

63. I will never allow fear, shame, guilt, anger, or past failures to prevent me from doing what is right by law and by my conscience.

64. I am the best thing that has ever happened to me, and I celebrate this fact every single day.

65. I am blessed with the body and mind of a goddess. I am endowed with features that pay homage to the deity within.

66. I am a talented woman with unique gifts and skills that make me a valuable addition to any organization or team.

67. Regardless of people's opinions, social conditioning, or personal circumstance, I choose to celebrate myself.

68. I am cultivating the right atmosphere for my confidence. I surround myself with positivity and excellence.

69. I am backing my dreams with the work needed to make them my reality.

70. I am not afraid to work and think outside the box. As long as it guides me to my goals, I am down for it.

71. I am boldly defying all the odds that have been stacked against me. I will win no matter what.

72. I recognize those who want my downfall no matter how well they disguise themselves. I recognize them and cut them off.

73. I am living my best life every day. My happily ever after is a continuous experience.

Closing

And just like that, we have come to the end of one phase of your journey. You know what they say, "the end of a book is the beginning of another." I personally don't believe in endings. I believe we simply transform. You started this journey with the objective of building up your confidence and changing your mindset. After 365 days of affirmation, there is no way you are the same person you were when you started this journey.

The transformation has begun, and it is your job to keep it going until you become the person you want to be and more. I may not be able to hold your hand and guide you through the next 365 days but know that I am rooting for you girl. I want to see you winning as a badass queen living and loving her life. I want to witness your awesomeness on full display for the entire world to see. You have such a bright light inside you and with your permission, the world will see it too.

You can choose to repeat the affirmations in this book for another year. You can make alterations to suit your narrative and expectations as you grow. Whatever you decide to do, ensure that you are consistent and committed in your affirmations. Keep your chin up. Hold your head high. And when those turbulent storms come your way, gently brush the dust off your melanated skin, do the fro flip and affirm you were born ready to face them. Don't forget; you are a Queen, and this life is yours to do with as you please.

Keep winning!

Thank You

Before you go, I just wanted to say thank you for purchasing my book.

There are many books on the same topic, but you took a chance and chose this one.

So, thank you for choosing me and for reading this book all the way to the end.

Now, I wanted to ask you for a small favor. **Could you please consider posting a review for the book? Reviews are the easiest way to support an independent author like me.**

Your feedback will help me continue to create books that will help you achieve the results you want. So, if you enjoyed it, please let me know.

Image - vecteezy.com